Extreme Coral Reef!

Q&A

Smithsonian | Collins

An Imprint of HarperCollinsPublishers

D0732061

CALGARY PUBLIC LIBRARY
OCTOBER 2008

Smithsonian Mission Statement

For more than 160 years, the Smithsonian has remained true to its mission, "the increase and diffusion of knowledge." Today the Smithsonian is not only the world's largest provider of museum experiences supported by authoritative scholarship in science, history, and the arts but also an international leader in scientific research and exploration. The Smithsonian offers the world a picture of America, and America a picture of the world.

Special thanks to Dr. Stephen Cairns, Curator/Research Scientist, National Museum of Natural History, Smithsonian Institution, for his invaluable contribution to this book.

Special thanks to Phillip Lobel, Professor of Biology, Boston University, for his invaluable contribution to this book.

This book was created by **jacob packaged goods LLC** (www.jpgglobal.com).
Written by: Melissa Stewart **Creative:** Ellen Jacob, Dawn Camner, Sarah L.Thomson, Andrea Curley, Louise Jacob, Brenda Murray

Photo credits: pages 4–5: © Susan Blanchet/Dembinsky Photo Associates; **inset:** National Oceanic and Atmospheric Administration/Department of Commerce; **pages 6–7:** © Mark M. Magner; **page 7:** © Jesse Cancelmo/Dembinsky Photo Associates; **pages 8–9:** © Marilyn & Maris Kazmers/Dembinsky Photo Associates; **page 10, both:** National Oceanic and Atmospheric Administration/Department of Commerce; **page 11:** © Mark M. Magner; **pages 12–13:** © APImages; **pages 14–15:** © Susan Blanchet/Dembinsky Photo Associates; **page 15 insets:** © 2007 JupiterImages Corporation; **pages 16–17:** © Jesse Cancelmo/Dembinsky Photo Associates; **pages 18–19:** © Russ Gutshall/Dembinsky Photo Associates; **page 19, inset:** © Brad McMahon; **page 20, both:** © 2007 JupiterImages Corporation; **page 21:** © Jesse Cancelmo/Dembinsky Photo Associates; **page 22, inset:** © Phil Degginger/Dembinsky Photo Associates; **pages 22–23:** © Jesse Cancelmo/Dembinsky Photo Associates; **page 24:** © Jesse Cancelmo/Dembinsky Photo Associates; **page 25:** © Susan Blanchet/Dembinsky Photo Associates; **pages 26–27:** © Mark M. Magner; **page 28:** © Jesse Cancelmo/Dembinsky Photo Associates; **page 29:** © Jeff Rotman/Photo Researchers, Inc; **page 30:** © Alexis Rosenfeld/Photo Researchers, Inc.; **page 31:** © 2007 JupiterImages Corporation; **page 32:** © 2007 JupiterImages Corporation; **pages 32–33:** © B. Jones/M. Shimlock/Photo Researchers; **page 34:** © 2007 JupiterImages Corporation; **page 35:** © 2007 JupiterImages Corporation; **pages 36–37:** © Jesse Cancelmo/Dembinsky Photo Associates; **page 38:** © APImages/Cayman Islands Dept. of Tourism; **page 39:** © APImages; **page 40:** © John Moore/APImages; **page 40, inset:** © Peter Scoones/Photo Researchers, Inc.; **pages 42–43:** © Alexis Rosenfeld/Photo Researchers, Inc.; **page 45:** Debe Tighe

The name of the Smithsonian, Smithsonian Institution and the sunburst logo are trademarks of the Smithsonian Institution. Collins is an imprint of HarperCollins Publishers.

Extreme Coral Reef! Q&A Copyright © 2008 by HarperCollins Publishers
Manufactured in China. All rights reserved. No part of this book may be used or reproduced in any manner whatsoever without written permission except in the case of brief quotations embodied in critical articles and reviews. For information address HarperCollins Children's Books, a division of HarperCollins Publishers, 1350 Avenue of the Americas, New York, NY 10019.
www.harpercollinschildrens.com

Library of Congress Cataloging-in-Publication Data
Extreme coral reef! Q & A. — 1st ed.
p. cm.
ISBN-978-0-06- 111575-2 (pbk.) — ISBN 978-0-06-111577-6 (trade bdg.) 1. Coral reef animals—Miscellanea—Juvenile literature. 2. Coral reef and islands—Miscellanea—Juvenile literature. 3. Coral reef ecology—Miscellanea—Juvenile literature. I. Title.
QL125.E98 2008 2007020895
591.77'89—dc22 CIP
AC

1 2 3 4 5 6 7 8 9 10 ❖ First Edition

Contents

This close-up view of orange cup corals shows their tube-shaped bodies and long, spiky tentacles.

Sometimes soft corals, such as this fan coral (left), and hard corals, such as this brain coral (right), grow side by side.

What is a coral animal?

Imagine a soft, tube-shaped creature about the size of a pencil eraser. One end is attached to a hard surface so the little animal won't float away. At the other end, a ring of tiny tentacles waves through the water. That's a coral animal, or a **polyp**.

Are all coral animals the same?

Scientists have discovered more than 5,000 **species**, or kinds, of coral animals in Earth's oceans. Certain coral polyps **absorb**, or take in, minerals such as calcium from the ocean water. They use the minerals to make limestone skeletons at the base of their bodies. Colonies of such polyps and their mineral base are called hard corals. Even dead coral skeletons keep the pattern or surface structure that is characteristic for each species and can be used for identification. Other species have polyps that make flexible, leatherlike skeletons and are called soft corals.

How do coral animals get their food?

Coral polyps usually go inside their skeletons during the day to avoid being eaten by **predators**, such as fishes. At night they stretch out their tentacles and catch tiny ocean creatures that drift by. Coral polyps sting the **prey** with specialized **cells** in their tentacles. Then they pull the food into their mouths.

Most of the coral polyps that live in shallow waters have another way of getting food. Millions of one-celled **algae** live inside each polyp. The algae and the polyp work as a team. Like plants, algae collect energy from the sun and use it to make food. But algae don't need all the food they make. The rest can be used by the polyp. Some polyps get most of their food from their algae partners.

In return a polyp provides a safe home for the algae. The algae also get important **nutrients** from a polyp's waste materials.

SMITHSONIAN LINK
Algae can be as small as a microscopic single cell or as large as foot-long seaweed. Learn more about this amazing group of creatures at the Smithsonian's "Algae Research" web page. www.nmnh.si.edu/botany/projects/algae

At night, the white tentacles of these coral polyps catch food as they sway through the water.

A polyp's algae partners do more than make food for the coral. They also give coral animals their bright, beautiful colors.

These star coral polyps are releasing eggs and sperm into the water.

Do coral animals live alone?

Some coral animals live alone, but most live in large groups called **colonies**. A coral colony grows as polyps split in half to form new polyps. This process is called **budding**. It is one of the ways polyps **reproduce**, or create more young polyps.

How else do coral animals reproduce?

The same corals can reproduce by releasing eggs and sperm into the water. This is called **spawning**. When an egg meets up with a sperm from the same coral species, they join to form a new cell. Eventually that new cell develops into a young coral, or **larva**. The larva can drift away from the parent colony. If it finds a good surface on which to settle, the larva will grow into a polyp. As that polyp buds, a new coral colony will begin to form.

What happens when coral animals die?

When polyps die, their skeletons are left behind. Sometimes new polyps anchor themselves to the old skeletons. Over time, hundreds of corals may grow on top of each other and form amazing structures.

Elkhorn coral (green) and clubtip finger coral (blue) are both hard corals.

What is a coral reef?

Coral structures come in all shapes and sizes. Soft coral colonies form shapes such as trees, fans, and feathers that sway with the ocean's currents.

A coral structure that includes layers of living hard coral polyps growing on top of dead leftover limestone skeletons is called a coral reef. Many kinds of coral colonies can grow together on a reef. Some are large and flat like tables. Others are branched like a deer's antlers. They can also look like fingers or dinner plates or even giant brains or giant mushrooms.

Pillar corals can be found on coral reefs just off the coast of Florida.

Look at the bright red sponge in the front of this photo. It's easy to see the sponge growing on top of the brown coral to its left.

Where are coral reefs located?

The polyps that form coral reefs can survive only in warm seawater. The algae living inside the polyps have specific needs too. To collect energy from the sun, they must live in clear, shallow water.

Only one part of the world has the temperature conditions and clean water that polyps and their algae partners need.

It is along continental coasts and around islands within a 3,000-mile band on either side of the **equator**, with the Tropic of Cancer as the northern border and the Tropic of Capricorn as the southern border.

Where are the world's largest coral reefs?

The Great Barrier Reef off the northeast coast of Australia is the largest group of coral reefs in the world.

It is more than 1,250 miles long and covers an area the size of New Mexico.

The second-largest barrier reef is off the coast of Belize, a country in Central America. The Smithsonian Institution has a research station on Carrie Bow Cay, a small island on top of the reef.

This is what Australia's Great Barrier Reef looks like from an airplane.

SMITHSONIAN LINK

Interested in the coral reef research happening right now at Carrie Bow Cay? Go to the Smithsonian's "Caribbean Coral Reef Ecosystems" web page.

www.mnh.si.edu/biodiversity/ccre.htm

How many different creatures can you spot on this coral reef? It's located just off the coast of Florida.

How is a coral reef like a city?

Coral animals aren't the only creatures that live in, on, and around a coral reef. Like a city, a coral reef is a crowded, busy place. Every inch of the reef is covered with life.

Sea turtles spend most of their time in the open ocean, but they often come to coral reefs to hunt for food.

Colorful fishes dodge and dart among the coral. Crabs and shrimp scuttle over the surface of the reef, while turtles and octopuses glide through the water. Worms and sea stars crawl among the seaweeds and seagrasses that sprout from the ocean floor.

Almost one-quarter of all known species of sea creatures depend on coral reefs.

Some groupers are more than three feet long. They usually feed on fish, octopuses, crabs, and lobsters.

Why are coral reefs so crowded?

A coral reef offers something that nearby open ocean waters can't—plenty of shelter and food. Shrimp and crabs hide from enemies in the reef's nooks and crannies. Clams and oysters anchor themselves to the reef's solid surface. Fishes rest under the reef's ledges or in its small caves.

Warm, shallow ocean waters contain almost none of the minerals, decaying plants, and other nutrients that sea creatures need to survive. The plants and animals living on a coral reef have to share the few precious nutrients available. As one animal eats another, nutrients move up the food chain. When animals release wastes, the nutrients help seagrasses and seaweeds grow. That means there will be more food for plant eaters. In this way, the reef's nutrient supply is always being recycled.

A coral reef near the Fiji Islands in the Pacific Ocean teems with life.

Are all coral reefs the same?

This coral atoll has a bright blue lagoon surrounded by reefs. It is off the coast of Belize.

Even though no two coral reefs are exactly alike, there are three main kinds of reefs. Scientists place coral reefs in these groups based on where they're located and how they formed.

- A fringing reef lies just off the shore of an island or coastline. The water between a fringing reef and the shore is shallow.
- A barrier reef lies farther offshore than a fringing reef. A **lagoon** (a shallow body of water) separates the reef from the shore.
- An atoll is a ring-shaped reef that surrounds a lagoon. The lagoon may contain many smaller reefs.

An atoll may be located far away from the mainland.

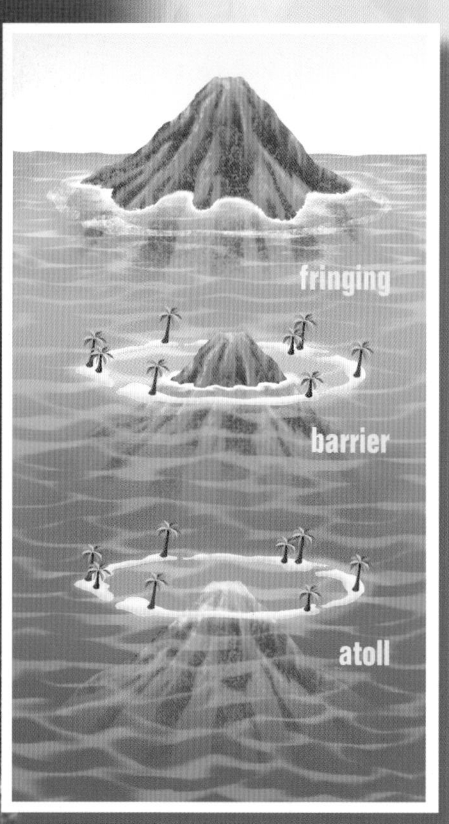

This diagram shows the three kinds of coral reefs—fringing reefs, barrier reefs, and atolls.

SMITHSONIAN LINK

The Smithsonian Institution's National Museum of Natural History is developing a new ocean exhibit. To learn more about it, take a look at its "Ocean Initiative" web page.
www.mnh.si.edu/ocean

What kinds of fishes might be seen on a coral reef during the day?

As the sun shines on a coral reef, a pair of colorful butterfly fishes probes crevices for algae and plankton. One nibbles on a coral polyp. Not far away, a poisonous boxfish dines on a worm. Its body is so well armored that only its mouth, eyes, and fins can move.

A bright orange seahorse looks up with one eye and down with the other. When the coast is clear, it swims out into the open and slurps up tiny shrimplike creatures drifting in the water.

A seahorse isn't a strong swimmer. When it wants to stay in one place, it wraps its tail around a coral structure and holds on tight.

Meanwhile, a triggerfish ripples its delicate fins to back out of a dead end. Then it grabs a sea snail with its thick lips and breaks open the shell with its strong jaws. Above the bigger fish and its prey, a giant manta ray glides through the water as it feeds on **plankton**.

A brightly colored manta ray glides through the water.

Butterfly fishes often travel in pairs.

Like its relatives the octopus and squid, the cuttlefish catches prey with its tentacles.

What else might be seen on a coral reef during the day?

While the fishes on a coral reef go about their business, a brightly colored nudibranch crawls along the ocean floor in search of sponges. Above it, a cuttlefish munches on a shrimp. If it feels threatened, it can change the color of its skin to match its surroundings.

On the other side of the reef, a ferocious mantis shrimp searches for its next meal. When it spots a snail, the hunter whacks the prey with its strong, clublike claw and cracks open the shell. Not far away, a clam rests on the ocean floor with it shell wide open.

A nudibranch has two tentacles that are orange and fingerlike. It feeds on sponges such as the three hole-covered yellow sponges near it.

It filters tiny creatures out of the seawater surrounding its body.

What kinds of fishes might be seen on a coral reef at night?

A coral reef is never completely quiet. As soon as butterfly fishes and seahorses, nudibranchs and mantis shrimp settle down for the night, other creatures wake up and swim out over the reef.

Squirrelfishes, cardinalfishes, and soldierfishes all have large eyes to help them see at night. During the day, they rest under ledges or in small caves. When the sun goes down, they come out to eat. While squirrelfishes scan the seafloor for crabs and shrimp, cardinalfishes munch on tiny creatures resting on the muddy bottom. Above them, soldierfishes gobble up small animals floating in the water. Any of these fishes would make a perfect meal for a hungry moray eel. These long, snakelike fishes hide in holes and ambush prey as it passes by.

During the day, this bright red fish would be easy to spot. But soldierfishes come out at night when they are almost impossible to see.

Even at night, a coral reef is full of life. In this photo, the light from a diver's headlamp reveals a lone squirrelfish.

Spiny lobsters don't have the big claws of Maine lobsters.

What else might be seen on a coral reef at night?

Fishes aren't the only coral reef creatures out at night. While a sea urchin munches on seaweed, a basket star perches on a colony of soft coral, spreads its spindly legs, and feeds on plankton.

Meanwhile, a worm burrows along the ocean floor, gathering tiny bits of food from the sand. Not far away, sluggish sea cucumbers suck up decaying materials.

As a red night shrimp races across a field of dead coral, a spiny lobster grabs it and gobbles it down. Next, the hungry predator sets its sights on a nearby clam. But before it can attack, an octopus swoops down and has the lobster for dinner.

SMITHSONIAN LINK
Ever wondered about the world's largest sea urchin or fastest sea star? Check out the Smithsonian's "Echinoderm World Records" web page.
www.nmnh.si.edu/iz/echinoderm/body_records.htm

As the sun goes down, red night shrimp come out by the thousands to feed.

A sea urchin's soft body is protected by its hard shell and long, spiky spines.

What are the busiest times on a coral reef?

A coral reef bustles with activity night and day, but the busiest times of all are dusk and dawn.

In the late afternoon, fishes feeding in open waters near the reef return for the night. At the same time, nighttime fishes leave their resting spots and swim out over the reef. The fishes change places again at sunrise.

As soon as one animal moves out of its hiding place, another moves in. Because creatures share caves and crevices, large coral structures can support an incredible number of fishes and octopuses, sea stars, sea snails, worms, crabs, and more.

A school of blackbar soldierfishes forms just after sunset.

In the late afternoon, fishes that are active during the day swarm around the reef looking for shelter.

Why do large predators go to coral reefs at dusk and dawn?

This shark knows that dawn and dusk are the best times to hunt on a coral reef.

Dawn and dusk are the perfect times to hunt. Sharks patrol the waters above the reef. They are looking for tired fishes returning to the reef or groggy ones just waking up.

Working in teams, hungry jackfish surround schools of small fishes and then go in for the kill. Moray eels hide in shallow caves and ambush fishes that have trouble seeing in the dim light.

A lionfish knows that most fishes follow the same routes to and from the reef every day. It waits among the coral for potential prey to pass by. Then it lunges at fishes and uses its long, winglike side fins to sweep a few into a corner. When the little fishes try to escape, the lionfish sucks them up in one giant gulp.

A moray eel darts out of its hiding spot.

SMITHSONIAN LINK

Carole Baldwin, a scientist at the Smithsonian Institution's National Museum of Natural History, had some exciting experiences with moray eels while diving off the Galápagos Islands. Read all about them in her online journal and Q & A page. www.mnh.si.edu/expeditions/galapagos/q-a.htm#11

How do some reef creatures help their neighbors?

You might be surprised to learn that some fishes and shrimp willingly swim right into the mouths of lionfishes, barracudas, and other ferocious predators. Why aren't they afraid of becoming fish food? Because they're performing an important service for the hunters.

Wrasses, gobies, and a few kinds of shrimp help reef fishes of all shapes and sizes stay clean and healthy. They eat the **parasites** that crawl on their neighbors' bodies and the bits of food that get stuck between their teeth.

Most coral-reef cleaners sport bright blue stripes and swim in a zigzag pattern. That's how other fishes know the cleaners are friends, not foes. When they see them, the fishes can line up and wait for their turn to get living toothpicks.

The bright blue stripes on the bodies of these fishes tell other reef creatures that they are cleaners.

Inside the large fish's mouth, a small cleaner fish hunts for bits of food that have gotten stuck between the larger fish's teeth.

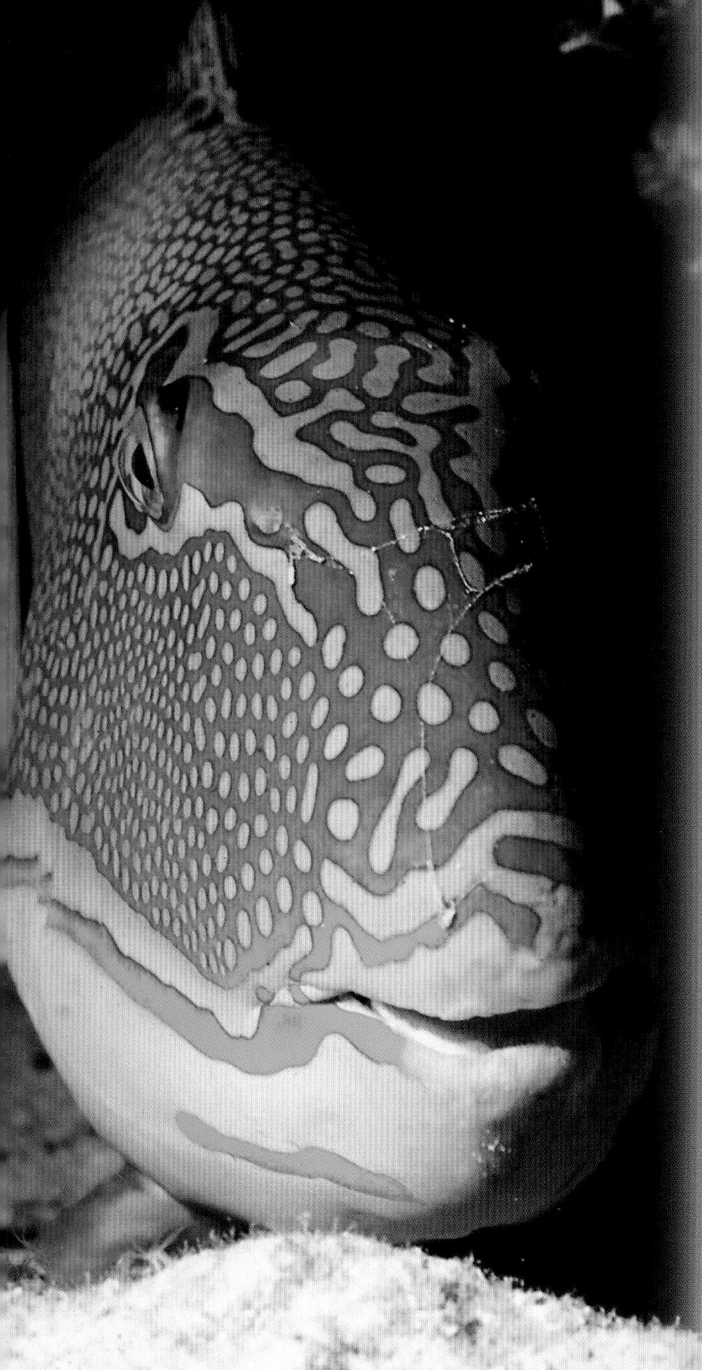

Why are parrot fishes important?

A parrot fish gets its name from its beak-shaped mouth. Its teeth are fused into a strong scraper that's perfect for knocking chunks of coral off the reef. What is the parrot fish really after? The algae inside.

Special bones in the fish's throat grind coral into sand. The sand travels through the fish's **digestive system** and leaves as waste material. Believe it or not, we have parrot fishes and other coral-crunching creatures to thank for many of the world's sandy beaches.

Parrot fishes all have a strong beaklike mouth but come in many colors and sizes.

How do clown fishes stay safe?

Like their coral relatives, sea anemones have stinging tentacles. Most fishes stay far away from an anemone's dangerous tentacles, but not clown fishes. Thick, sticky **mucus** protects their bodies from the anemone's sting.

When predators threaten clown fishes, they dart to safety among an anemone's tentacles. In return, clown fishes chase away some of the butterfly fishes that feed on anemones. Anemones may also get nutrients from food bits and waste dropped by clown fishes.

Most clown fishes are identical—orange with white stripes and less than five inches long.

How do coral reefs help people?

People depend on coral reefs in many ways. Reefs protect islands and coastlines from giant storm waves. In some parts of the world, coral-reef fishes and shellfish are an important source of food.

Islands in the Caribbean Sea and Indian Ocean rely on their coral sand beaches to attract

This scuba diver is enjoying the beauty of a coral reef in the Red Sea.

visitors. Many countries with coral reefs depend on money brought in by tourists who snorkel and scuba dive.

Coral reefs are an important source of medicines. Chemicals from reef creatures have helped scientists create drugs to treat asthma, heart disease, ulcers, and cancer. AZT, a drug used to treat AIDS, comes from a sponge that lives on Caribbean reefs.

Are coral reefs in danger?

Hurricanes and tidal waves can harm coral reefs, but these natural disasters don't cause nearly as much damage as people do. Even though coral reefs help us, we do many things that make it hard for them to survive.

How do tourism and fishing harm coral reefs?

Tourists can damage coral reefs by collecting coral or accidentally stepping on it. When boat anchors bang into coral, reefs may break apart.

A group of scuba divers prepares to descend to a coral reef in the Caribbean Sea.

Overfishing can disrupt coral reef food chains. If there are no fishes to eat seaweed, it may grow too quickly and smother corals.

Some fishers blow up coral reefs to make it easier to drag fishing nets through the water. People who catch reef fishes for aquariums may use poisonous chemicals. The chemicals stun the fishes, so they are easier to collect.

The fishes recover, but they usually die a few months later.

These divers are repairing and cleaning coral on the Sudbury Reef, one section of Australia's Great Barrier Reef. The reef was damaged when a cargo ship struck it in 2000.

Building developments like this one along Mexico's Caribbean coast can harm coral reefs.

This example of bleached coral was photographed off the Maldive Islands in the Indian Ocean.

How do construction and pollution harm coral reefs?

When people build houses or hotels on the coast, rain can wash soil into the water and make it cloudy. Then the corals' algae partners can't collect energy from the sun. If the algae die, so do the corals.

Water pollution, such as chemicals from household cleaners and oil from roads, can make corals weak, so they have trouble fighting diseases. Some water pollution is full of nutrients. The nutrients can make seaweeds and seagrasses grow so quickly that they smother coral.

How can rising sea temperatures hurt coral reefs?

Global warming threatens coral reefs by raising the temperature of the world's oceans. Hurricanes and other unusual weather events can also raise the temperature of ocean water. When seawater gets too warm, the corals' algae partners can't survive inside the coral. Algae give corals their beautiful colors. Without algae, corals turn white and usually die. Scientists call this coral bleaching.

SMITHSONIAN LINK
Visit the National Museum of Natural History's "IZ Facts" web page to learn more about corals and coral bleaching.
www.nmnh.si.edu/iz/cnidarians.htm

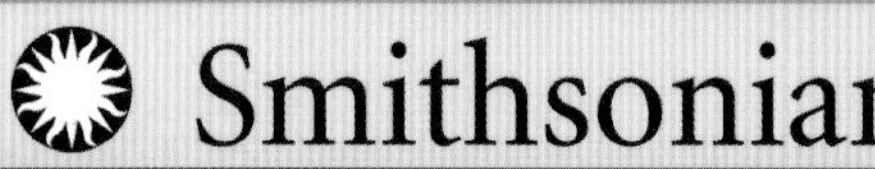

This diver is a scientist observing the creatures that live on this coral reef so he can help protect them.

What can we do to save coral reefs?

Scientists and people who work for environmental organizations are trying hard to save coral reefs. They teach tourists and schoolchildren to respect the reefs and treat them with care. They urge everyone not to keep coral-reef fishes in home aquariums and not to buy shells and corals collected at coral reefs.

More than fifty countries have created **reserves**, or protected areas, around coral reefs. People can't fish in reserves, and tourists need special permission to scuba dive there. The Northwestern Hawaiian Islands Marine National Monument is the largest ocean reserve in the world.

Governments of some countries are working to slow global warming. They have passed laws that will reduce the amount of pollution released into the air.

Scientists are studying reefs so we can understand them better. The more we know about coral reefs, the easier it will be to make good decisions about protecting the creatures that live there.

Dr. Stephen Cairns
CURATOR/RESEARCH SCIENTIST,
NATIONAL MUSEUM OF NATURAL HISTORY

Why did you become a zoologist?

When I was ten I decided to become a marine biologist and I never changed my mind. At that time, I lived in a coastal town in Cuba, near wonderful sandy beaches. My mother and I would walk along the beach and snorkel in the water, collecting seashells and other marine animals.

What do you do most of the time?

Most of my time is spent looking at coral skeletons under various microscopes, studying the literature for previous descriptions of coral species, and writing up my results. I often refer to papers published as far back as 1758, because you don't want to repeat something that was already done before. Scientists can learn a great deal, but if they do not share this information with others, then all that information is almost useless.

Where do you do your research?

My research is done at the Smithsonian Natural History building in Washington, DC, but about once a year I use a three-man research submersible to see how deep-water corals live in their natural habitat. Sometimes we go down about a mile, where there is no light at all, the water is quite cold outside, and the water pressure is enormous.

Do you travel in your job, and if so where?

Every curator must do fieldwork to study his or her animal or plant group. It is one of the nice bonuses of being a naturalist. I have been on oceanographic cruises to the Hawaiian and Galápagos islands and to Australia, New Zealand, Africa, Brazil, the Caribbean, the Philippines, and Panama.

What new technology has helped you most with your job?

For me, the invention of the scanning electron microscope opened up a whole new world for me. This microscope allows me to see parts of corals at up to 10,000× magnification and even allows me to view the object in stereo. For the first time I have been able to see new structures that help identify and classify various coral species.

Is there something in your field you wish was studied more?

Corals occur in quite deep water, as deep as 4 miles. In fact, more than half of the 5,000 species occur deeper than 150 feet. Only about a dozen scientists in the world, including me, study the classification of deep-water corals.

What do you like most about your job?

One of the most exciting things about my job is discovering a new coral species and determining how it is different from all other species. Along with this discovery comes the responsibility of naming the new species, a task that I have done over three hundred times. And, yes, I have named a coral species after my wife.

Glossary

absorb—To take in.

alga (pl. algae)—A simple aquatic plant, generally known as seaweed. Algae can be as small as a microscopic single cell or as big as 12 inches long.

budding—The process by which some creatures reproduce by splitting in half.

cells—The basic building-block unit of every living organism. There are trillions of cells in the human body.

colony—A group of animals that live and grow together.

digestive system—The organs in the body that break down foods, release nutrients into the blood, and get rid of wastes.

equator—An imaginary line around the middle of Earth, at a right angle to the axis of rotation; it divides Earth into northern and southern halves (hemispheres).

lagoon—A shallow body of water.

larva—In some animals, young that hatches from an egg and later changes its form to become an adult.

mucus—A thick, sticky material. It coats the scales of some fish. Mucus protects clown fishes from the sea anemone's stinging tentacles, and it protects some kinds of fish from parasites.

nutrient—A chemical in food that living things use to build body parts. Minerals, vitamins, proteins, and sugars are all nutrients.

parasite—A creature that lives on or inside another creature and feeds on it.

plankton—The collection, in high numbers, of small plant and animal life that floats or swims weakly on or near the surface of water.

polyp—A coral animal.

predator—An animal that hunts and kills other animals for food.

prey—An animal that is killed and eaten by another animal.

reproduce—To create young.

reserve—A natural area that is protected by law.

spawning—When a female animal releases eggs and a male animal releases sperm in the same place at roughly the same time.

species—A group of creatures that share certain characteristics. The members of a species can mate and produce healthy young.

More to See and Read

Websites

There are links to many wonderful web pages in this book. But the web is constantly growing and changing, and we cannot guarantee that the sites we recommend will be available. If the site you want is no longer there, you can always find your way to plenty of information about coral reefs through the main Smithsonian website: www.si.edu.

Learn more about coral reefs and coral reef creatures.
www.coralfilm.com/index2.html

Find out how groups of children and adults are working together to save coral reefs.
www.coralreef.org

Take a look at Ocean World's "Animal, Mineral, or Vegetable?" page for great information and photos of corals.
http://oceanworld.tamu.edu/students/coral/coral1.htm

The Reef Education Network features fun facts, activities, and fantastic photographs of coral reefs.
www.reef.edu.au

Suggested Reading

At Home in the Coral Reef by Katy Muzik, illustrated by Katherine Brown-Wing

Colorful Captivating Coral Reefs by Dorothy Hinshaw Patent, illustrated by Kendahl Jan Jubb

Coral Reefs by Sylvia Earle, illustrated by Bonnie Matthews

Hello Fish! Visiting the Coral Reef by Sylvia Earle, photographed by Wolcott Henry

One Night in the Coral Sea by Sneed B. Collard III, illustrated by Robin Brickman

What Lives in a Shell? by Kathleen Weidner Zoehfeld, illustrated by Helen K. Davie

What's It Like to Be a Fish? by Wendy Pfeffer, illustrated by Holly Keller

Index